How to
YodEL

Lessons to Tickle Your Tonsils

How to YodEL

Lessons to Tickle Your Tonsils

Wylie Gustafson

ILLUSTRATIONS BY ROBERT PAUL PAYNE

Gibbs Smith, Publisher

TO ENRICH AND INSPIRE HUMANKIND

Salt Lake City | Charleston | Santa Fe | Santa Barbara

First Edition
11 10 09 08   5 4 3 2

Text © 2007 Wylie Gustafson
Illustrations © 2007 Robert Paul Payne
Photographs © 2007 as noted on page 95
Cover photograph © 2007 Bill Watts

Published by
Gibbs Smith, Publisher
P.O. Box 667
Layton, Utah 84041

Orders: 1.800.835.4993
www.gibbs-smith.com

Recordings on CD included with this book.
CD Recordings © Two Medicine Music BMI

All songs and instructional segments written by Wylie Gustafson. Not to be duplicated or copied without written permission.
Two Medicine Music
24502 SR 127
Lacrosse, Washington 99143
E-mail: yodeler@pionnet.com

Designed by Dawn DeVries Sokol
Printed and bound in Wisconsin

Library of Congress Cataloging-in-Publication Data
Gustafson, Wylie.
  How to yodel : lessons to tickle your tonsils / Wylie Gustafson ; illustrations by Robert Paul Payne. — 1st ed.
    p. cm.
  ISBN-13: 978-1-4236-0213-2
  ISBN-10: 1-4236-0213-7
  1. Yodel and yodeling—Methods—Self-instruction. I. Title.

MT893.G87 2007
783.9—dc22
                              2007009193

To my mother and father,
Pat and Rib Gustafson

Contents

CD Contents

Acknowledgments

I'd like to acknowledge and thank the real music lovers of the world and "commercially averse" listeners who have made it possible for me to have an unlikely career as a cowboy singer and professional yodeler. Without a willing and appreciative audience, a yodeler would not have a reason to emerge from practice sessions in the shower.

Also, thanks to my mother and father. I have been blessed with a loving, nurturing, and creative set of parents who *never once* tried to dissuade me from wandering down the uncertain path of becoming a professional musician. What a wonderful trip it has been.

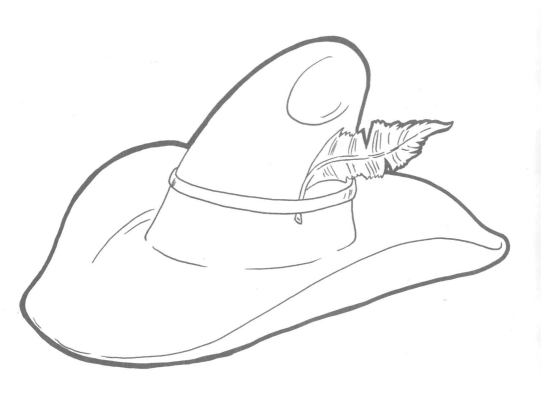

Disclaimer

I, nor the publishers of this book, will be responsible for the consequences resulting from techniques used in this book, including:

Stampeding buffalo
Frightened pets and children
Avalanches
Disappearance of friends
Stock market surges
Marital discourse
Tectonic shifts
Feelings of euphoria
The swallows not returning to San Juan Capistrano

oooo!

Welcome all of you musical rebels and melodic daredevils. Congratulations on taking your first step toward becoming the world's next vocal virtuoso, Pavarotti of the plains, epiglottis goddess . . .

YODELING SUPERSTAR!

You have taken a left instead of a right down a road less traveled—but a heck of a lot more interesting. This book will help feed that gnawing hunger of those who seek adventure. By immersing yourself in these simple lessons, you will find the heartfelt affection of adoring fans and lovesick coyotes!

Aren't you the one who has the urge to use the door that says "exit only"? Or drive a bit faster than the speed limit indicates? Yodeling could very well be the outlet that your untamed soul has been yearning for, the mud that your inner ducky has been craving. Click off the TV, power down the computer, and get ready to add some good-old-fashioned-fun to your life in a totally legal way. Perhaps you just want to impress your next date. Maybe you have visions of giving your acceptance speech at the Grammy award podium next to Snoop Dog and the Rolling Stones.

As a child I found myself in the unfavorable position of being the youngest of five siblings. If I wanted any attention I had to make myself heard! Dad gave me the key to being noticed when I heard him yodel from atop the

hill as he prepared to dive his skis into deep powder.
Wow! I was hooked.

From that day on I practiced, crooned, yowled,
and shouted my way through my awkward teenage
years. My schoolmates thought I was cool . . . but
maybe one joker short of a full deck. Yodeling turned
out to be a pretty good way to get some recognition
in the fragile social climate of junior high.

As I grew older and started playing in bands, I
learned a yodeling song called "Louisiana Lady" by
the country rock group New Riders of the Purple
Sage. That song was the first of many yodeling songs
that entered my repertoire as a professional singer. In
the mid-1980s I lived in Los Angeles while pursuing
my recording career. It was in the City of Angels that

I started combing through the bins at used record stores. In the dusty and dark confines of those archives of sound, I discovered the musical treasures of Jimmie Rodgers, Elton Britt, Kenny Roberts, and Slim Whitman, to name a few. These masters from the forgotten heyday of professional yodelers were some of my earliest influences. In 1989, I wrote my first yodeling song: an autobiographical ditty called "The Yodeling Fool." It is still one of my most requested songs to this day.

While living in Los Angeles, I was discovered by an audio production company that specialized in creating the audio tracks for nationally televised advertisements. I sang yodels for Mitsubishi, Miller Lite, Porsche, and Taco Bell and others to help

Never underestimate the power of a yodel!

promote their products. In 1996 a small and relatively unknown company named Yahoo! needed a yodel for one of their first commercials. They wanted something that would catch listeners' attention. I spent about ten minutes in the studio and laid down several short yodels. Little did I know that one of my yodels would become one of the most widely heard audio logos of the century. The moral of the story? Never underestimate the power of a yodel!

There are several "how to yodel" books and CDs on the market. The purpose of this book is to teach you the *basics* in a fun and informative way. Hopefully, my method will give you a touch of warbling fever and within a short time have you belting out the kind of yodel that would make a

Bavarian goatherd happy to know you. By following along with the CD included in this book, you will find that anyone with the will to persist can master the basic yodel. I have purposely not focused on the super fancy, pyrotechnical-type yodels as they take much time, perseverance, and monkey grease to master. My goal is to help you understand the funda- mentals and create the solid foundation needed to excel in the art of yodeling. If you discover that you enjoy yodeling and its outlet of creative release, I urge you to search the reference materials in the back of this book. Go further and develop a style that fits you.

Good luck. Have fun. Be cool. And welcome to the wonderful world of yodeling!

To Sing Is Fine . . .
To YODEL Is Divine

Can anyone yodel?

I have been asked that question countless times. My answer? You bet! If you can talk, you can yodel.

Considered a novelty by some, yodeling has a rich and vibrant history. From being a language of alpine goatherds to a calling card of modern day cowboy singers, it is a sound that refuses to go away. In fact, it has grown and blossomed into a dynamic art form.

Contemporary yodeling and its many styles can be heard in the repertoires of many of today's musical artists. As one of those artists, I have personally witnessed the *power* of the yodel. There is nothing more rewarding than watching the faces of listeners light up when they hear what the human voice is capable of through the art of yodeling.

In 1830 Sir Walter Scott opined that yodeling was a "variation on the tones of a Jackass." Indeed, yodeling has suffered some negative publicity in its colorful past. But to hear a good yodeler bust out a yodel is an otherworldly feeling of which there is no comparison. Yodeling can energize the soul and elevate the spirit. Perhaps it was the inspiration for King David to write in Psalm Ninety-Eight of the Bible: "Shout for joy to the Lord, all the earth, burst into jubilant song with music."

23

So What THE HECK Is a Yodel?

According to Merriam-Webster:

Main Entry: **yo·del**

Pronunciation: 'yO-d$^{\&}$l

Function: *verb*

Inflected Form(s): **-deled** *or* **-delled**; **-del·ing** *or* **yo·del·ling** /'yOd-li[ng], 'yO-d$^{\&}$l-i[ng]/

Etymology: German *jodeln*

intransitive verb : to sing by suddenly changing from a natural voice to a falsetto and back; *also* : to shout or call in a similar manner

transitive verb : to sing (a tune) by yodeling

— **yo·del·er** /'yOd-l&r, 'yO-d$^{\&}$l-&r/ *noun*[1]

[1]Merriam-Webster Online Dictionary. 2007. http://www.merriam-webster.com (30 April 2007).

24

According to Wylie:

Merriam-Webster gives you the technical definition of yodeling. What it doesn't touch on is the importance of "soul" needed to bring the yodel to life. The soul is the personal character that we all have, the individual attitude that we exude when we talk or sing. Yodeling is no different. You see, it is not so much about hitting all the right notes at all the right intervals. Sometimes the magic of the yodel will be the sheer happiness we impart on an upbeat yodel romp, or the sadness we exude when we swoop up to pluck the ethereal high notes of an alpine lullaby. *Soul* is the unquantifiable part of the whole yodel equation. After you master the basics of the yodel, don't forget to give it life by imparting a little bit of your unique self.

> The soul is the personal character that we all have, the individual attitude that we exude when we talk or sing.

YODEL History 101

Musicologists and cultural theorists have attributed the yodel to many different origins. Some say it is the alpine inhabitants' vocal reflection of their native geography (with the high peaks and low valleys). Others claim that it all started when singers tried to emulate the tone of the alphorn or other early day instruments. Was it man's aural response to the lonesome coyote? There have been purported connections to man's primal scream or call of love. Perhaps it was the shepherd's need to communicate to his herd or fellow herders. I believe the elements of yodeling have been derived from a multitude of sources and reasons. Most likely, it crept into our world via the human need to emote and express oneself through sound and song.

The alpine style of voice breaking has been the biggest influence on today's most popular forms of yodeling. Alpine yodeling began as a type of communication between folks who lived valleys apart. Originally, this art form was known as *Juchzin*, short yells with different meanings such as "bring in the goats" or "Hey there neighbor, let's go grab a triple mocha latte at Starbucks!"

So how did yodeling end up in American music? No

> The alpine style of voice breaking has been the biggest influence on today's most popular forms of yodeling.

"Bring in the goats!"

one knows for sure, but there are a
few theories. The U.S. is known for
its mish-mash of cultures. Most likely someone early on figured out that
yodeling sounded pretty good
in an upbeat western tune. Maybe it
was the same person who figured
out that french fries taste pretty
good with ketchup.

Most likely
someone early on
figured out that
yodeling sounded
pretty good in an
upbeat western tune.

Here is a story I once heard about how yodeling
came to be in western music: In the 1930s, a swing
band from the Oklahoma/Texas area featured a singer
who was born and raised in Austria. One night the
lead fiddle player called in sick. In the fiddle player's
absence, the singer who dearly missed his alpine

homeland improvised yodels for the sections of the songs that were in need of a solo.

Another theory on the origins of yodeling in cowboy music is revealed in the lyrics of the song "That's How the Yodel Was Born":

The bronco jumped and the cowboy came down
They met at the old saddle horn
It made a deep impression
You could say it changed his life
And that's how the yodel was born.

From the song "That's How the Yodel Was Born," written by Douglas B. Green. 1979 Songs of the Sage (BMI). Used with kind permission.

31

OTHER LESS POPULAR THEORIES ON THE ORIGIN OF YODELING

- Caveman sitting on a yucca plant
- Family dog's response to hearing contestant on *American Idol*
- Tarzan's attempt at opera
- Milk cow stepping on the Swiss farmer's foot

Section 2:

Let's
do iT!

It's time for all of you closet yodelers and secret admirers of the falsetto flip to take a step forward. This is your moment to grab life by the tail and reach for the stars. It's time to let the world know just how weird you really are. Some folks have a tendency to be a little boring, but you were meant to march to the beat of a different accordionist. It's time to let loose those surly bonds that have chained you to the drudgery of a yodel-free existence. Your desire to learn to yodel is a good thing!

The answer to unlocking the gate to the verdant pastures of your creativity lies within the pages of this section. Here you will learn that yodeling is more than an exercise in vocal dynamics—it is also a mindset! I have never known a yodeler who didn't have a pretty good sense of humor. Learning to yodel should be more than just a little bit fun. Save your more serious attitude for when you try out for first violin in the Boston Philharmonic.

Just think, *you* could be the next vocal superstar of the new millennium . . . or the best shower singer this side of the tracks. The urge to be heard is nothing new. Mankind has been yelping, howling, and singing to the moon for the last twenty thousand years. It's time to go for it. It's time to yodel!

> Learning to yodel should be more than just a little bit fun.

A DOZEN GOOD REASONS TO YODEL

1. Yodeling is uber-cool.
2. It's good cheap fun.
3. Chicks dig yodelers.
4. Your worst day yodeling is still better than your best day at the DMV.
5. You only live once.
6. Your voice is your instrument—no harmonicas or pianos to lug around and you won't have to keep forking out fourteen bucks for a set of guitar strings.
7. Yodelers never have to experience the humiliation of bovine indifference.
8. Yodeling makes wearing lederhosen totally appropriate.
9. Learning to yodel is a self-lesson in humility.
10. Yodeling can prepare you for a career as a cough drop salesperson.
11. What else do you have to do with your time?
12. When you yodel, you **will** be heard, dang it!

Show Biz Secrets for Yodelers

Big Secret #1

Rome wasn't built in a day. You can learn the basic elements of the yodel in a matter of minutes. But proficiency in yodeling, like everything else, takes practice. It's like learning a new language—it doesn't happen overnight. Yes, you may be born with a little more (or a little less) talent than your neighbor, but the bottom line holds true: *The quality of your yodel depends heavily on the amount of time you invest in practicing.*

> The quality of your yodel depends heavily on the amount of time you invest in practicing.

The key to making your first public foray into the world of yodeling a success is "KISS": Keep It Simple, Stupid! Start with the easy yodels and master them before you move on to the more complicated yodels. Jimmie Rodgers made a career out of simple yodels. For Jimmie, the key to making it work was keeping it simple. Don't be tempted to move on to the thornier stuff until you have the basics mastered. There is a beauty in the simple yodel that often gets overlooked. Don't be tempted to automatically

> Start with the easy yodels and master them before you move on to the more complicated yodels.

Johnny Weissmuller
was the Austrian-born
actor who made the
Tarzan yodel famous.

39

go for the fancy, pyrotechnical, acrobatic stuff. Experiment and have fun trying to stretch your limits, but be aware of your boundaries. Make sure you master the simple yodels before moving on to the fast and the furious.

Big Secret #3

The key to making yodeling work for some audiences is understanding its power. The "If a little is good, then a lot must be better" philosophy doesn't necessarily apply to yodeling. Use the yodel judiciously—don't hit folks over the head with it. In other words, stringing three upbeat barn burners together may be sensory overload for many listeners—*especially if it is not done expertly.* There is a subtle and dynamic approach to yodeling that needs to be understood and respected.

Corollary #1 (also known as Show Business Rule #1): Always leave the crowd wanting more.

Big Secret #4

Finding the right key to yodel in is paramount in delivering a good yodel. Nothing ruins a yodel like trying to hit notes that are out of your natural range. So what is your natural range? For every person there is a perfect key to sing in. And the perfect key will change from person to person, male to female, child to

Finding the right key to yodel in is paramount in delivering a good yodel.

adult, baritone to tenor. That is why we have different key signatures for songs. Any song can be transposed to a different key to fit the voice of the singer. Unfortunately when sheet music is written, the editor has to choose a key and hope that it will fit the singer.

For the musically unsophisticated, we can find our natural range by singing along with a song and finding that we don't have to strain to hit any of the notes. For the more musically advanced (those who know how to play an instrument), we can change or transpose the key of the song we are playing until it fits our range.

In the instructional CD that comes with this book, I will play songs in two different keys. It is your job to find the key that works better for you.

The key to creating a quality yodel is in the "break" or transition from low to high voice. A seamless and natural-sounding break is what makes a good yodel sound so beautiful. Remember how Mr. Haney from the TV show *Green Acres* or the pimple faced teenager from *The Simpsons* talks? That is a natural voice break.

Your regular/chest voice is the voice you use in everyday conversation. Go ahead and count to ten out loud while resting your fingers on your throat. Now sing "Mary Had a Little Lamb." Notice where the vibrations and sound are originating from—they should be coming from the area around the back of your throat and chest.

The voice of Mickey Mouse is a man speaking in falsetto, or his head voice. Women can speak in a falsetto voice also. To switch to your falsetto voice, simply go up to a higher, "false"-sounding voice. Now count to ten out loud while resting your fingers on your throat. Sing "Mary Had a Little Lamb" again. Do you notice that the vibrations have diminished from your throat area? With your falsetto voice you should be using your nasal cavity to produce the sound. We'll practice finding your voice break a little later on Track 3 of the CD.

Big Secret #6

Don't take yourself too seriously . . . because your audience may not either.

45

WHERE SHOULD ONE PRACTICE YODELING?

As with beginning fiddlers, flugelhorn players, and harmonica blowers, it may be in your best interest to practice out of earshot of your friends, roommates, family members, and sensitive pets. Seriously, if you don't have to worry about others listening to your first attempts at yodeling, you will progress quicker and build the confidence needed to crank out a bold yodel. A few ideas for where to practice:

- In a truck, by yourself, with the windows rolled up
- High atop the Matterhorn
- On a wild bucking bronco
- At the end of an airport runway
- At a NASCAR race
- On a sailboat in the middle of the Great Salt Lake
- In the heart of the Gobi Desert
- On an iceberg in Antarctica
- In a hot air balloon at 5,000 feet

WHERE NOT TO YODEL

- Confession
- Funerals
- A marriage proposal
- The library
- A chess tournament
- The movie theater
- Corporate meetings
- During the SAT

- At your niece's first piano recital
- After downing the last wiener at a hot dog eating contest
- On the eighteenth green at the PGA Masters

49

Yodeling is not kind to those who can't be limber and relaxed.

Relax

Yodeling is not kind to those who can't be limber and relaxed.

The physics of a successful yodel demand that your vocal muscles be loose and lithe rather than pumped up tighter than Ahnold's pecs. The trick to a great yodel is a smooth and seamless transition from your chest voice to your head voice.

It is easy at first to try too hard and be a little tight and nervous. Pick a spot to practice where you won't be worried about others listening to you. And don't worry too much about sounding really bad at first. My mom had to shut the door to my bedroom quite often when I was in the heat of a self-taught yodeling lesson. Any good yodeler has to start somewhere, and most of us start out sounding less than perfect.

How to relax? Find a nice, soft place to lie down and take some easy, deep breaths from the area of your midsection between your chest and stomach. Feel the air rise in and out, but don't force it. Do this for a few minutes before you try to sing. Relax your mind. Think of the most peaceful place on earth you have ever been. Now, let your mind take you back to that place. Once you are there, you will be ready to stand up and begin your lesson.

Any good yodeler has to start somewhere . . .

MORE WAYS TO PREPARE FOR A BEAUTIFUL YODEL

- Gargle with lukewarm saltwater
  with a dash of lemon
- Think of green alpine pastures filled
  with blissful sheep
- Take a hot aromatic bath
- Listen to an iPod crammed with Enya tunes
- Sip a tall glass of good wine (21 years or older, please)
- Remember your first kiss
- Become a yoga master

Let's Yodel!

Now that you're completely relaxed, it's time to grab the CD enclosed in the back of this book and follow along. In this section and on the accompanying CD, I will give you exercises to practice the voice break, teach you a basic yodel, and let you try your hand at different yodeling styles. I'll also teach you some tricks you can do to add panache to your yodeling.

I have purposefully stayed away from musical charts and notation because I truly believe that you will learn faster and be more creative if you aren't "fenced in" by the rigid structure of sheet music. All of the yodelers I know (including myself) have learned to yodel by listening to and imitating their favorite yodelers or recordings. Good yodeling will be an exercise in improvisation of sounds and notes based on your mood and personality. Okay—let's plug in the CD and get started!

Track 1
Welcome

The Basics

This first set of lessons will teach you the basics of yodeling and how to find your natural range.

Track 2
Voice Warm-Ups and Breathing Exercises

Your voice is created by using the muscles of

your diaphragm and lower throat to create vibrations. So it makes sense to do some vocal calisthenics before we start. In this lesson we will also try to find our natural voice break.

> The "Yodel" mixed drink . is made of Fernet Branca liqueur, orange juice, and sparkling water.

Track 3
Finding the
Elusive Voice Break

In this lesson, you will practice the octave swoop and will work on finding your voice break.

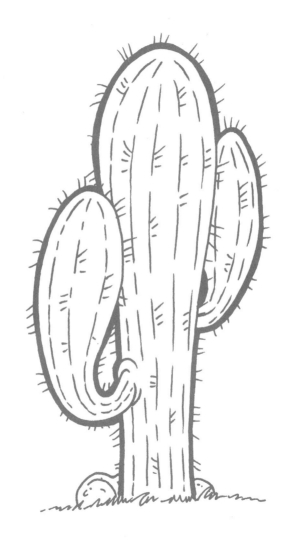

Track 4
Knock Knock Yodel

This lesson will teach you the classic knock knock joke.

Track 5
Triad Yodel

The triad yodel is a basic three note yodel that is the foundation of the western yodel.

There are certain vowels that work well together, like "ay" and "eee" (as in "tree"), or "oh" and "ooo" (as in "cool"). We'll stick with the simple stuff to start.

Track 6
Advanced Triad Yodel

Here, we will spice up the triad yodel by adding words.

Track 7
Finding Your Natural Range

Here are some examples of triad yodels in different keys. Follow along with me and my guitar to find where it is most comfortable for you to yodel.

> There are certain vowels that work well together, like "ay" and "eee."

The bark of the
Basenji dog is
eerily similar to
Jimmie Rodgers's
blue yodel.

Do It Your Way

This next set of lessons will teach you yodeling styles. In American music there are different styles of yodeling just like there are different styles of music in general. Part of the fun of learning how to yodel is finding a style that fits you. I have included the basics to a few of the most popular styles of yodeling. Try to find your best yodeling style!

Yodeling styles include:

Cowboy Fast or Slow—à la Emmett Miller, Roy Rogers, Kenny Roberts, Wilf Carter, Patsy Montana. Usually features entire solos or sections of yodeling.

> Part of the fun of learning how to yodel is finding a style that fits you.

61

Every June, over
fifteen thousand
professional yodelers
turn out to stretch
their vocal chords at
Switzerland's biggest
Jodlerfest, held in Biel,
Switzerland.

Most Recorded Yodel Song:
"She/He Taught Me How to Yodel"

Blue Yodeling—à la Jimmie Rodgers. A simple style that involves using the yodel as a refrain or to add color to the end of a verse or chorus.

Voice Break Yodeling—à la Hank Williams, Slim Whitman, Emmett Miller. Following a melody while alternating between regular and falsetto voice. Voice break songs include "Indian Love Call," "Lovesick Blues," and "The Lion Sleeps Tonight."

Swiss or Alpine—à la masters Franzl Lang and Peter Hinnen. Classical European yodels.

Track 8
Fast Cowboy Yodel

Here we speed things up a bit to get you on your way to being the next Roy Rogers.

Track 9
Blue Yodel

This is a lesson in the blue style of yodeling where we will add a yodel at the end of a verse for character à la Jimmie Rodgers.

Track 10
Voice Break Yodel

We will practice a style of yodeling that follows a melody as opposed to the triad yodel.

Track 11
Slow Lullaby Yodel

Tune into this lesson to learn the "voice break" style of yodeling to a slow waltz beat.

Track 12
Swiss Yodel

This is a lesson in the European alpine style of yodeling.

Adding Some Color to Your Yodel

This final set of lessons will teach you some fancy tricks—the icing on your yodeling cake, if you will.

Track 13
Tongue Tricks

Using your tongue to create trills is a simple way to dress up a yodel. We will start by going through some simple tongue exercises. I will then show you how to incorporate tongue techniques into your yodel.

Track 14
Voice Break Rhythms

We will start with some simple, slow voice break rhythm exercises. I will then show you how to incorporate them into your yodel.

Track 15
Conclusion to the Lessons

Thanks for following along with the instructional CD!

TOP TEN YODELING HITS

1. She Taught Me How to Yodel
2. Cattle Call
3. I Want to Be a Cowboy's Sweetheart
4. Chime Bells
5. Lovesick Blues
6. T for Texas (Blue Yodel #1)
7. I'm Casting My Lasso towards the Sky
8. Indian Love Call
9. The Lion Sleeps Tonight
10. My Little Swiss Miss

The first recorded yodel occurred around 1895. The song was "Sleep Baby Sleep."

Songs of Wylie & the Wild West

Now, for more practice (and for your listening pleasure), I have included three songs I have written that are recorded on our album *Bucking Horse Moon*, released in 2007. After each song is a version without vocals so you can try your luck at karaoke yodeling.

Track 16: Whip out a Yodel (with vocals)

"Lovesick Blues" has been sung by the likes of Emmett Miller, Patsy Cline, Glen Campbell, Slim Whitman, Jerry Lee Lewis, Linda Ronstadt, Don McLean, and George Strait. But the most well-known version was recorded by Hank Williams (right) in 1948.

Track 17: Whip out a Yodel (without vocals)

Track 18: Eltopia Yodel (with vocals)

Track 19: Eltopia Yodel (without vocals)

Track 20: Uber Yodel (with vocals)

Track 21: Uber Yodel (without vocals)

> I did pretty good
> for a guy who never
> finished high school
> and used to yodel at
> square dances.
>
> —Roy Rogers

World's Largest Group Yodel:
1,773 Yahoo! employees set the world
record by yodeling for over a minute on
November 20, 2003.

World's Longest Yodel:
In 1978 Donn Reynolds set the world record
for the longest yodel by yodeling nonstop for
seven hours and twenty-nine minutes.

Yodel·oh·OOO·TEE!

The World's Fastest Yodel:
In 1992 Peter Hinnen yodeled twenty-two tones
in less than one second for the
GUINNESS BOOK OF WORLD RECORDS.

> This song is Copyrighted in U.S., under Seal of Copyright # 154085, for a period of 28 years, and anybody caught singin' it without our permission, will be mighty good friends of ourn, cause we don't give a dern. Publish it. Write it. Sing it. Swing to it. YODEL IT. We wrote it, that's all we wanted to do.
>
> —WOODY GUTHRIE, SPEAKING ABOUT "THIS LAND IS YOUR LAND"

Happy Trails!

Yahooooo! You have now completed my carefully constructed tome, *How to Yodel: Lessons to Tickle Your Tonsils.* And you will be a better person for it, I'm sure! "The world needs more yodelers" is my motto—and hopefully yours too. You have not only learned a new way to express your inner self, but you have contributed to our American heritage by keeping a lost art form alive and kicking.

In addition to yodeling, the Unspunnen Festival in Switzerland features traditional Swiss folk dancing, alphorn playing, and the great sport of stone throwing.

One of your duties as a graduate of this instructional course is to spread the gospel of yodeling throughout the cultural wastelands of America. Okay now, young grasshopper . . . let the hills ring with the sound of yodeling!

"Coming up next: Can yodeling cure cancer? Of course not."

—NEWS ANCHOR KENT BROCKMAN ON The Simpsons

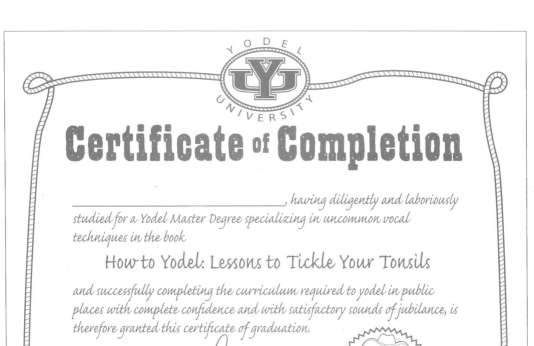

Certificate of Completion

_____, _having diligently and laboriously_
studied for a Yodel Master Degree specializing in uncommon vocal
techniques in the book

How to Yodel: Lessons to Tickle Your Tonsils

and successfully completing the curriculum required to yodel in public
places with complete confidence and with satisfactory sounds of jubilance, is
therefore granted this certificate of graduation.

_____
President of Yodel University
Wylie Galt Gustafson

WYLIE'S ELEVEN FAVORITE YODELERS

1. Sourdough Slim: A contemporary "old-time" accordion-playing cowboy singer from California. Sourdough Slim specializes in the yodeling style of the 1930s and '40s and is a favorite at the cowboy gatherings of the West.

2. Ranger Doug: Known as the "Idol of American Youth," Ranger Doug sings in the famous cowboy harmony group Riders in the Sky. He is the writer of "That's How the Yodel Was Born."

3. Elton Britt: Nicknamed the "World's Highest Yodeler," Elton Britt is one of America's most commercially successful and best-known yodelers. His career spanned from the 1920s through the 1960s. He sang several yodeling duets with Rosalie Allen and had minor hits with "Chime Bells" and "Skater's Waltz."

4. Kenny Roberts: This "King of the Yodelers" is one of the great original American yodelers. Also known as "Jumpin'" Kenny Roberts, he has been performing since 1943.

5. Roy Rogers (b. Leonard Franklin Slye): Rogers was one of the founding members of the Sons of the Pioneers who went on to a stellar career in Hollywood as one of America's favorite "good guys." He was one of the smoothest yodelers of all time.

6. Franzl Lang: Lang is the great European yodeler whose other-worldly sounds have brought the art of yodeling to a most sophisticated level.

7. Wilf Carter: Also known as "Montana Slim," Carter is a Canadian-born yodeler and Alberta cowboy.

8. Slim Whitman: America's best-known "pop" yodeler, Whitman had several yodeling hits, including "Indian Love Call" and "Rose Marie."

9. Kerry Christensen: This "master yodeler" specializes in alpine styles and is a favorite at Octoberfests.

10. Patsy Montana (b. Ruby Blevins): Montana was the first female country singer to sell a million records with the yodeling standard "I Wanna Be a Cowboy's Sweetheart."

11. Jo Miller: This Seattle-based yodeler once fronted "Ranch Romance" and currently fronts the "Burly Roughnecks."

Glossary

alphorn—A natural wooden horn having a cup-shaped mouthpiece, used by mountain dwellers in the Alpine region of Europe.

blue yodel—A style of yodel derived from the African-American vocal style. This type of yodel is generally used as a simple refrain at the end of a verse.

chest voice—Natural tone created by using the lower range of the voice, which resonates in the chest.

diaphragm—A shelf of muscle extending across the bottom of the ribcage.

falsetto—A high-pitched voice used to reach the singer's treble range. The literal translation of *falsetto* is "false soprano." The technique can be used in speaking or singing and uses the breath in the frontal sinuses to produce a high tone.

head voice (also head register, falsetto)—a resonance of singing originating from the frontal sinus folds. Using this voice will feel to the singer as if it is occurring in his or her head.

range—The span from the highest to the lowest note a particular voice can produce.

triad yodel—A three-note yodel based on three distinct tones, built from thirds (third intervals).

voice break—The transition from chest voice to head voice. A smooth and effortless break should be the goal when yodeling.

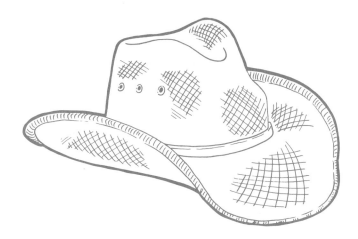

Resources

Audiovisual Recordings

Wylie & the Wild West. *Bucking Horse Moon.* Dualtone Records, 80302-01259-2. Compact disc.

———. *Hooves of the Horses.* Dualtone Records, CD 80302-01163-2. Compact disc.

———. *Ridin' the Hiline.* Rounder Records, CD3168. Compact disc.

———. *Paradise.* Rounder Records, CD3178. Compact disc.

———. *Way Out West.* Rounder Records, CD3152. Compact disc.

———. *Total Yodel.* Rounder Records, CD3162. Compact disc. [all yodeling songs]

Britt, Elton. *The RCA Years.* BMG Special Products, CD #CCM-031-2. Compact disc.

Christensen, Kerry. *U 2 Can Yodel.* Compact disc. [instructional CD]

Clark, Slim. *Yodelin' Slim Clark.* Old Homestead Records, #OHCD-4015. Compact disc.

Cotton, Carolina. *Yodeling Blonde Bombshell Vol. 1.* Kit Fox Records, CD #KFCD001. Compact disc.

Hudelson, Rusty and Tania Moody. *Duet Style Yodeling.* Videocassette.

Ranch Romance. *Western Dream.* Sugar Hill, #SH-CD-3799. Compact disc. [female yodeling & yodeling harmonies]

Riders in the Sky. *Yodel the Cowboy Way*. Rounder Records, CD#7055. Compact disc.

Roberts, Kenny. *Indian Love Call*. Starday, #SCD-336. Compact disc.

Rodgers, Jimmie. *The Essential Jimmie Rodgers*. RCA, #67500-2. Compact disc.

Schneider, Mary. *Yodelling the Classics*. Dino Records, #DIN420D. Compact disc. Australia release.

Slim, Montana. *Dynamite Trail*. Bear Family Records, #BCD 15507. Compact disc.

Various Artists. *American Yodeling 1911–1946*. Trikont Records, #0246-E/U. Compact disc.

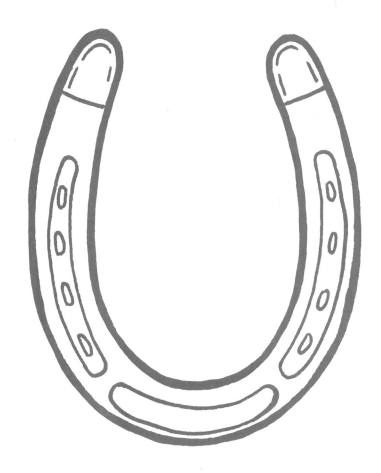

Various Artists. *The Greatest Yodelling Album of All Time.* Rajon Entertainment, #RJBOX51. Compact disc.

Various Artists. *Yodelling Crazy.* EMI Records, CDP 7986562. Compact disc.

Various Artists. *Yodelling Mad.* Jasmine Records, JASMCD 3552. Compact disc.

Whitman, Slim. *Vintage Collections.* Capitol Records, #7243-8-54321-2-5. Compact disc.

Books

Fink, Cathy and Tod Whittemore. *Learn to Yodel.* Homespun Tapes, 1985. Booklet with two compact discs.

Plantenga, Bart. *Yodel-Ay-Ee-Oooo: The Secret History of Yodeling Around the World*. New York and London: Routledge, 2004.

Robbins, Ruby and Shirley Field. *How to Yodel the Cowboy Way*. Centerstream/Hal Leonard, 1997.

Web Sites

Yodel Central
www.spidra.com/yodel.html

Yodel Course
This site teaches yodeling of the Alpine variety.
www.yodelcourse.com

Yodelers

Wylie Gustafson, Wylie & the Wild West
www.wyliewebsite.com, yodeler@pionnet.com

Kerry Christensen
www.kerrychristensen.com

Yodel·ay·HEE·Hoo!

Jo Miller
www.burlyroughnecks.com

Riders in the Sky
www.ridersinthesky.com

Rusty Hudelson and Tania Moody
www.yodelers.com
888-266-5569

Slim Clark
PO Box 100
Brighton, MI 48116

Sourdough Slim
PO Box 2021
Paradise, CA 95967
530-872-1187
www.sourdoughslim.com

Photo Credits

page 70
Courtesy Hank Williams Museum, Montgomery, Alabama

page 80, top right
Vern Evans

page 80, bottom left
Jim McGuire

page 81, top right
From the author's personal collection

page 81, bottom left
Courtesy Kenny Roberts

page 82
Used by permission of the Roy Rogers-Dale Evans Happy
    Trails Theater and Attraction in Branson, Missouri.

page 83
Courtesy Jo Miller

Yodel·ay· EEE·TEE!